The Finality of Jesus Christ

THE FINALITY OF JESUS CHRIST

EXPLODING THE MANY-ROADS-TO-GOD MYTH

JIM ANDREWS
JULI ANDREWS GROSE

Truth Encounters Publishing
Portland, Oregon

CONTENTS

Acknowledgements

We, the authors, would like to express our extreme gratitude to Jimmy Park for producing the first edition of *Finality*. Jimmy and his wife, Ivo, have given their selfless and energetic service to the Lord in many ministries.

We would also like to thank the following people for their invaluable contributions, without which this project would have never come to fruition. These folk utilize the skills and gifts God gave them to partner with us, in spirit of Philippians 1:5, to spread the Gospel to the glory of God.

Paul Grose was editor-in-chief for the project, coordinating with us and supervising all aspects of production. Lynne Mackey formatted the book for this second edition with her usual talent for beautiful layout. Mari Kaeding designed and created the new front and back cover, and Brian Overholt developed the graphics for the inside pages. Ross Crowley made it possible for people to purchase this book on www.jim-andrews.org. And finally, Jan Van Horn, Rita Hughes and others proofread the manuscript. We are deeply indebted to these members of our technical team.

ONE WAY >

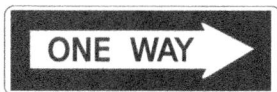

Introduction

Today, many people share the opinion of the famed Mahatma Gandhi, who reportedly remarked that God has no religion, meaning that, with God "any dab will do ya." However, on what basis did Gandhi have the authority to pontificate about such matters? Of course, I have no clue, since these matters are well beyond his knowledge, and he had no benefit of divine revelation.

Such is the arrogance of modern man.

Years ago, a lady (I'll call her Mary—not her real name) who had just begun attending our church scheduled an appointment to talk to me about spiritual issues. Of course I was happy to oblige.

When we met shortly thereafter, she described herself as an earnest seeker. Indeed, she appeared to be a very sincere, intelligent lady with honest questions.

Mary related to me a life trauma that had disoriented her spiritually and then had eventually led her to us. She expressed her initial relief and delight to "at last encounter someone who stood for something." Yet later, she lamented that during communion the previous Sunday, her hope of finding what she was seeking had been shaken. For during that monthly observance, I had declared sweepingly that Jesus was "the way and the truth and the life," emphasizing to boot that "no one comes to the Father except through [Him]" (John 14:6) [NIV, brackets mine].

"At that point," she related, "I was so disappointed. I more or less just kind of slumped in my seat … I had always believed that there were many ways to God."

To Mary, my remarks about the finality of Christ as the one and only divinely acceptable approach to God came across as narrow-minded, though she was too kind and diplomatic to put it that bluntly. It was hard for her to fathom how I could hold allegiance to Jesus Christ as the only approved pathway to the Father. Isn't that being exclusive toward unbelievers? Why would God be so inflexible? And, by the way, how did God accept those who lived before Christ came? What about those reared in non-Christian cultures who never had an opportunity to receive or reject Christ? Wouldn't that, in effect, condemn the adherents of other religious traditions who refuse to acknowledge the God of the Bible as the one true God and Jesus Christ as *the* Lord and Savior? Was it fair of God, she wondered, to punish people such as these?

These were all valid and significant questions.

This allegedly exclusive aspect of the Gospel message is a sore point with many non-Christians. Always has been. Always will be. Some of our theology at this point simply mystifies people (as in the case of Mary). Others it infuriates.

So here, we begin to expound upon Mary's first two questions, **"Is there *really* only one way to God? Isn't that being exclusive?"**

Let me deal with the second question first. The term, "exclusive," may be misleading. Why? Because *anybody* can come to God. For the Apostle Paul teaches us in Romans 10:13 that the invitation is open to all, "… WHOSOEVER WILL CALL UPON THE NAME OF THE LORD WILL BE SAVED" [italics mine]. So then, the welcome mat is extended to all people universally. What *is* exclusive is the *way* of salvation. It is exactly like buying bread. Anybody is welcome to purchase it. The store is not a private club. However, the item can be purchased only on the store's terms. They, for example, accept only American currency, not Monopoly money. So, it is the *means* of salvation that is exclusive, <u>not</u> the invitation. This is because, as the Apostle stated above under the inspiration of the Holy Spirit, God welcomes all men to receive the gift of salvation, which is available to *everyone*, but only on the basis of faith in Christ alone.

However, in this climate of arbitrary political correctness and muddled postmodern thinking (in which pluralism is "In" and truth as a fixed, objective entity is "Out," especially in religious and moral matters), many see one's religious beliefs as something considerably less consequential than matters of life and death. To these people, the world is a mall of religious boutiques. Curiosity in religion is chic. Religious options are much like a spiritual cafeteria where culinary choice is no big deal ... simply a matter of personal taste and cultural preference. To unbelievers, it's totally annoying when we Christians come along, like the functional equivalents of militant environmentalists, and insist that the choice is not so benign as all that ... that in fact, figuratively speaking, the decision comes down to a fateful choice between healthful, life-giving cuisine and toxic fare that ultimately kills its consumers.

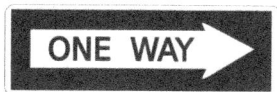

The Scriptures: Our Supreme Court

Two Ways to Approach the Question

Before I address other issues that Mary raised, we must understand that there are only two ways we can approach her first question: **Is there *really* just one way to God?** First, we can merely speculate about spiritual reality by believing and promoting what seems right in our own eyes (Judges 21:25). Or, we can ground our conclusions on biblical teaching—that is, God's revealed message through His prophets and apostles. Historic Christianity considers this message to be absolutely authoritative when it comes to faith (what we believe) and practice (how we act) because it has been revealed by our Creator.

This first option, human speculation, is an intellectual dead end ... a dead end because the subject matter is transcendent, which means that it is well beyond the competence of unaided human reason to determine. So, speculative thinking about such theological matters is about as enlightening as two blind men arguing about the colors of a rainbow.

Thus, all you get is a fact-free clash of discordant voices from opinionated people (such as Gandhi) speaking in cadences that make them sound more knowledgeable than they really are. The fact is, coming from this position, they know absolutely nothing—zero—concerning the theological matters about which they confidently speak. Why? Because, as we pointed out earlier, they have no authority upon which to base their conclusions. For apart from God's revelation, such answers are inaccessible and little more than vapors of intellectual gases.

So then, the Bible has to be our *starting point* in any theological question. As orthodox Christians, we affirm the Scriptures as the repository of what God has chosen to reveal to man. But why do we so adamantly adhere to such a proposition? It is because this foundational premise is not based on a so-called leap of "blind" faith, as some think; rather, it is a theological position derived from evidence *within* the Scriptures and strongly supported by evidences *external* to it. For example, the Scriptures are replete with detailed prophecies written hundreds of years before their fulfillment. The fact that these predictions predate the fulfillment of the specified historical events is verified by scholars the world over.

Perhaps one of the most poignant prophecies is Isaiah 53, in which the prophet predicts the suffering, crucifixion and resurrection of Jesus Christ. Without question, scholars confirm the ancient date of this passage to be at least 700 years before Christ. And the same is true for prophecies of Christ's crucifixion and resurrection in Psalms 22 and 16, written by King David a thousand years before the events.

Moreover, in New Testament (NT) times, there were hundreds of people who witnessed the very events Isaiah and David prophesied about Christ. And these events were recorded within a generation of their actual occurrence, not only preventing the possibility of legends developing, but verifying the mindboggling accuracy of such predictions. Those are just *some* of the reasons (among many others) why we treat the Bible as our "supreme court." Thus, our position is that whatever the Bible teaches, God teaches, and that is the end of the discussion.

Naturally then, we Christians are obliged to conform to what the Bible prescribes for our beliefs and practice, just as our civil government, in all its arms and agencies, is bound to conform to the principles and prescriptions of the U.S. Constitution.

The Old Testament Verdict: Designer Religion Unacceptable

Therefore, since the Bible is our starting point in *any* theological question, it is thus inconceivable that anyone at all familiar with biblical literature could postulate that God "puts out the welcome mat" for people to approach Him any way they please. From the standpoint of biblical theology, such a view is as intellectually absurd as the weird notions of the Flat Earth Society.

If there is one motif that resounds all through the Old Testament (OT) like an echo in a canyon, it is this: *God's creatures will approach Him in His way or no way.* That was the recurring message of all the biblical prophets. And this message is that the Judeo-Christian God forbids any rivals. It is intolerable for the God of Abraham, Isaac and Jacob, who is also the God and Father of our Lord Jesus Christ, for men to worship any god other than Himself. This law is literally etched in stone in the first of the Ten Commandments:

> You shall have no other gods before [that is, besides] Me. (Exodus 20:3) [brackets mine]

Furthermore, Israel's prophets condemned her repeated forays into religious pluralism as provocations against His holiness (that is, His transcendence and moral purity). The prophets also charged Israel with apostasy, which means a turning away from God. This apostasy exposed the nation to divine indignation and the unsparing rod of God's judgment.

Not only that, but the covenant that Yahweh (God's self-revealed name that means "I am who I am") formed with Israel at Sinai strictly regulated her forms of worship. Her carefully circumscribed rules and rites of worship were intended, in part, as a safeguard against the infiltration of her pagan neighbors' customs of worship.

So, God is by no means indifferent to religious pluralism. He does not honor such diversity. For the way people approach God makes a statement about who they believe God is, what He is like, and what His purpose is for His creatures. Religion either exalts God or degrades His Name (that is, His character) by misrepresentation.

Thus, the Law and the Prophets underscore the fact that Israel's holy God can be safely approached by sinful men only on His terms. *How* one worshipped God was (and is) as important as *which* god one served. That point is evident from the second of the Ten Commandments (Exodus 20:4-5) that demands:

> You shall not make for yourself an idol, or any likeness of what is in heaven above or on the earth beneath or in the water under the earth. You shall not worship them or serve them; for I, the Lord your God, am a jealous [possessive] God, visiting the iniquity of the fathers on the children, on the third and the fourth generations of those who hate Me" ["hate" as evinced by their rejection

of His commandment and presumption in offering Him unauthorized worship]. [brackets mine]

Therefore, we see that God abominates the tendency of mankind to misrepresent His Being. From time immemorial, sinful humans have persisted in their efforts to reinvent the God who is really there. But He detests it when men recast Him in a morally deformed character more comfortable to their own darkened desires. Repeatedly, the story line in OT narratives illustrates the judgement men bring upon themselves when they serve Yahweh according to their own desires, falsify His nature and character, and even worship other gods. To fail to observe this OT principle would be as amazing as visiting the Grand Canyon and missing the view.

In summation, from the Ten Commandments *alone*, it is plain that the God of the OT countenances no rivals and that He takes serious offense at religious knock-offs and any form of "designer" religion. He obviously regards these "alternative" forms of worship as nothing less than iniquity (morally twisted behavior). God holds those who dabble in idolatry accountable for their slander.

The New Testament Verdict: Christ Is the Doorway of Salvation

Now let's turn to the witness of the New Testament.

The thesis that "designer" religion is acceptable to God is an intellectual nonstarter in the NT as well. If there is one message that resounds through the NT, it is that no one can bypass Jesus Christ and be received by God.

Consider, first, the doctrinal truth that my friend Mary heard me declare at the communion table. Actually I was quoting Jesus Himself. In John 14:6, Jesus announced to His disciples:

> I am the way and the truth and the life. No one comes to the Father except through Me. [NIV]

Could any biblical statement be clearer? Certainly His apostles got the message. Take, for example, Acts 4:12. When the Apostle Peter was on trial for healing a lame man in the name of Jesus, he was filled with the Holy Spirit and declared to the Sanhedrin (the Jewish senate, in effect) these words:

> … there is salvation in no one else; for there is no other name under heaven that has been given among men by which we must be saved.

So much for the "any-size-fits-all" theory of religious efficacy!

And what was plain to Peter was no less clear to the Apostle Paul. He, too, dispels the illusion that God allows man to choose from, as we said before, a "cafeteria menu" of many religious choices, none fatal but all efficient for getting their adherents to the same goal. How could the finality of Christ in the redemptive equation be put any more boldly than the following citation?

> For there is one God, and **one mediator** also between God and men, the man Christ Jesus, who gave Himself as a ransom for **all** … (1 Timothy 2:5-6a) [bolding mine]

Think about what the Apostle is saying. There is *only one* Mediator between our fallen race and God the Father. That go-between, Paul emphasizes, is Jesus Christ and Him alone.

Obviously, if mankind did not require a mediator, why would Jesus have offered Himself as "a ransom for all"? If salvaticn were accessible by alternative means, why would Christ have volunteered to endure the shame and horror of the Cross? If there were other ways to God, Jesus' so-called "ransom" would have been totally superfluous. And if unnecessary, thus foolish, not to mention masochistic, beyond words.

Now, should someone propound any other explanation for why Christ died on the Cross, this text forbids that too. For the Apostle "nails it down" for all time—Christ "gave Himself *as a ransom*." So let's shed any ideas that maybe His death was *just* a political murder (it was that, but much more), or perhaps a heroic example of dedication to God, or a noble gesture of dying to self, etc. No, His death was first and foremost "a ransom"—a payment to redeem lost, guilty but repentant souls from the penalty of their sin.

In addition, the picture of the awful doom that awaits those who reject Christ is graphically related by the Apostle Paul in 2 Thessalonians 1:6-10a, where he talks about the divine retribution that awaits those who persecute the followers of Christ:

> … [God] will pay back trouble to those who trouble you and give relief to you who are troubled, and to us as well. This will happen when the Lord Jesus is revealed from heaven in blazing fire with his powerful angels. He will punish those who do not know God and do not obey the gospel of our Lord Jesus. They will be punished with everlasting destruction and shut out from the presence of the Lord and from the glory of his might on the day he comes to be glorified in his holy people and to be marveled at among all those who have believed. [NIV, brackets mine]

It will not do to dismiss the Apostle as deceived or delusional concerning his stern warning. In either case, one is saying that Christian theology, based heavily on apostolic witness and teaching, is bogus. In fact, some unbelievers also attempt (vainly), during every Christmas and Easter season, to falsify the truths of historical Christianity. Why is it, then, that these same unbelievers swell up with indignation and charge Christians with narrowness, intolerance and bigotry when we expose the lethal errors of *their* false religions? Of course, this reveals their hypocrisy; they never think about the fact that *somebody* has to be wrong. Two incompatible and/or contradictory teachings cannot be correct—unless there is a "god" for whom anything goes.

The finality of Christ breaks through once again in the Apostle Paul's powerful argument in Romans 9-12. With profound anguish, he grieves over his Jewish countrymen, who had rejected Jesus as their Heaven-sent Messiah (or Christ). His people, Paul laments, had rejected God's way of righteousness; instead, they had gone about setting up their own religious standard. In other words, they sought God's approval through a merit-based system rather than receiving God's grace through faith in Christ's atoning sacrifice alone as a covering for their sin. Ironically, he notes, the pagan Gentiles, who weren't even "in the market" for a righteous standing with God, found it by receiving Christ's imputed (transferred) righteousness. Meanwhile, Israel zealously pursued its own works-based "righteousness" and therefore missed the mark (Romans 9:30-31).

How does one explain this anomaly? Well, in Romans 9:30-10:4, Paul explains that Israel:

> ... not knowing about God's righteousness [that is, not understanding what God requires to be accepted and how that acceptance is obtained] and seeking to establish their own [form of righteousness], they [the people of Israel] did not subject themselves to the righteousness of God [which is imputed through faith in Christ and not based upon legal merit]. (10:3) [brackets mine]

Think about the implications of that.

If there were many ways to God, Israel's refusal to receive her Messiah by God's prescribed method would not even be an issue. If, as the saying goes, there is more than one way to skin a cat, then surely first-century Judaism would have been the first to qualify as an alternative, since God had chosen them as a nation to be His representatives on earth. For, as Paul himself testified from personal experience, "... they [referring to his countrymen] have a zeal for God" (10:2a). But there was one significant disqualifying circumstance: Paul contends that their approach is simply "not in accordance with knowledge" [that is, the approach God had prescribed through revelation] (10:2b) [brackets mine]. However, Israel at this crucial point was lethally ignorant of the demands of her own God! And this ignorance was *culpable* because they had allowed layers of religious tradition and spiritual pride to obscure the light of divine revelation. Israel just didn't get it. And God was having none of it. Religious, yes, they were. Righteous, no. And that's fatal for both Jews and Gentiles.

Ah! Right there, we see that religious zeal and sincerity are no "safety nets" after all. God accepts only religion that is right, informed, and agreeable to His character and purposes; He rejects religion that is dead wrong, ill-informed, and disagreeable to His moral nature and will.

Therefore, the Apostle prays for his countrymen's salvation. For, until they repent (that is, change their minds and turn away from sin) and get on God's page, they remain lost and will surely perish.

Nothing about that has changed in 2,000 years. There was (and is) only one way of salvation, and it runs directly through Jesus Christ and the Cross.

But understand this: Our message is, by no means, in the proud, gloating spirit of a taunt. We are not self-righteous people who, like members of an exclusive private club, boast as though salvation is reserved for us and no one else. *Not at all* the case. Rather, as ambassadors of God, we extend to all people His gracious invitation: this salvation is available to you, and you, and you—and all others as well. Yet, we reiterate, faith in Jesus Christ is the only currency in God's kingdom. Substitute certificates and counterfeit coins are unacceptable.

There is, the Bible teaches, a Heaven to be gained, a Hell to be shunned; a Savior to be received, a judgment to be faced.

> He who believes in the Son has eternal life; but he who does not obey the Son will not see life, but the wrath of God abides on him. (John 3:36)

So, we see that trusting in God's Son alone for our salvation is the crux of the matter. The fate of every person on earth will hinge on this question: "What did you do with My Son?" No amount of religion of any kind, sincere or insincere, formal or informal, will save the person who refuses Jesus Christ. That is the ultimate slap in the face to God the Father, who sent Christ to redeem us. For Jesus said:

> … He who believes in Me, does not believe in Me but in Him who sent Me. (John 12:44)

We could probably leave it there, but let's drive a few more "NT nails" in the coffin of any theory that claims that there are other ways to God.

In his Mars Hill address to the Athenians, the Apostle Paul declares:

> … [God] has fixed a day in which He will judge the world in righteousness through a Man [Jesus] whom He has appointed, having furnished proof [of His credentials] to all men by raising Him from the dead. (Acts 17:31) [brackets mine]

If one religion is as valid as another to obtain a relationship with God, why would He call upon the men of Athens (as well as others) to repent of their pagan religiosity and to turn to Christ, the Lord and Judge of all:

> … God is now declaring to men that all people every-where should repent. (17:30b)

If their religion had been acceptable to God, why ask them to repent for their idolatry? Why mess with what isn't broken?

And who can evade the words of the Apostle John, who redlined the exclusive claims of Jesus' teaching in John 3:16-18:

> For God so loved the world, that He gave His only begotten Son, that whoever believes in Him shall not perish, but have eternal life. For God did not send the Son into the world to judge the world [that is, the first time around], but that the world might be saved through Him. He who believes in Him is not judged [condemned by God]; **he who does not believe has been judged already, because he has not believed in the name of the only begotten Son of God.** [bolding and brackets mine]

Obviously, men cannot reject Christ with impunity. God allows no "end runs" around His Son.

Now, why is it *so* damning to reject Christ in favor of man-made or "do-it-yourself"' religions? Just this, John says next:

> This is the judgment [that is, the basis of the divine condemnation], that the Light is come into the world [in the person of the Son of God], and men loved the darkness rather than the Light [Christ, whom God sent into the world as a litmus test of the moral and spiritual dispositions of the race], for their deeds were evil. For everyone who does evil hates the Light [and naturally recoils, by reflex, from it], and does not come to the Light [of Christ] for fear that his deeds will be exposed. (3:19-20) [brackets mine]

Wow, there's a statement! John blows away all religious and intellectual pretense. Even though unbelievers insist that they reject Jesus Christ only for intellectual reasons, ultimately, this is never the case. Naturally, they feel better about themselves if they can say that the claims of Christ are unreasonable to them. But, actually, that's just a high-sounding excuse. When you get to the bottom of it, the real reason for their aversion to Christ is essentially *moral*. People want to continue to live in sin because their moral affinity, like a colony of bats, is for darkness.

Though Light has come into the world (in the person of Jesus Christ), the greater mass of mankind rejects that Light. It repels them. To admit that, however, would be an act of self-condemnation. So we have these little intellectual charades. But God is not fooled about the motives and dispositions of rebellious humans, even if people have fooled themselves.

And He is not about to exonerate them, religious though they may be.

Lastly, in the sweeping summary statement quoted earlier, John "nails to the wall" the finality of Jesus Christ as the only way to God for all time:

> He who believes in the Son has eternal life; but he who does not obey the Son will not see life, but the wrath of God abides on him. (John 3:36)

And these are just a few extracts of New Testament testimony. The NT repeatedly teaches that Christ is the one and only avenue of salvation. One who argues with this fact arrogantly sets himself above the Scriptures. Of course, such people have no scruples about such impudence against their Creator. But for those of us who rest our theology on the Bible as the final arbiter of true doctrine, there is no escape clause. Jesus Christ is "**the** way and **the** truth and **the** life" (John 14:6a) [NIV, bolding mine]. No one comes to the Father except through Him (14:6b). His very own words. End of argument.

If we stand on biblical authority, it should now be beyond dispute that God does not exempt anyone—neither Hindus, nor Muslims, nor Buddhists, nor Jews, nor New Agers, nor Baptists, nor Methodists, nor Presbyterians, nor Catholics, nor pastors, nor priests, nor Mormons, nor Jehovah's Witnesses, nor self-righteous environmentalists—from this redemptive imperative: "… Believe in the Lord Jesus Christ, and you will be saved …" (Acts 16:31). Again, one comes to God His way or no way.

Some time ago, a staff member from our church was listening to a local radio program. The host and his guest were discussing a recent religious conference in Oregon connected with the (infamous) Jesus Seminar. The "theologians" at this seminar pawn themselves off as "scholars" whose ideological mission is to debunk the Jesus of the Bible.

According to this staff member, the guest on the show made a statement to this effect:

> Even most Christians today have come to realize that, if non-Christians are faithful [presumably to their own brand of religion], God is there for them too.

Well, it *is* true that God is there for everyone. In fact, the Apostle Paul proclaims this in Romans 10:11-13:

> … "WHOEVER BELIEVES IN HIM [Christ] WILL NOT BE DIS-APPOINTED." For there is no distinction between Jew and Greek; for the same Lord is Lord of all, abounding in riches for all who call upon Him; for "WHOEVER WILL CALL ON THE NAME OF THE LORD WILL BE SAVED." [brackets mine]

Indeed, He is the God of all living creatures and invites them to return to Him for salvation, but I repeat, always on His terms. And Jesus Christ is, if you please, the only password by which anyone enters heaven.

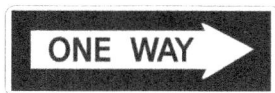

ONE WAY

The Savior: Our Singular Substitute

Why Would God be So Inflexible?

At this point, maybe we should answer another of Mary's questions: **Why must one pass only through Christ in order receive salvation?**

A simple answer *could be* that a sovereign God has that right. After all, the terms and conditions of acceptability for salvation are strictly at His discretion. The Scriptures teach us that He is beholden to none of His creatures (Ro. 3:23, Ro. 9:14-21).

By way of contrast, the faulty mindset of unbelievers is illustrated in one of John Wayne's great westerns. In *Rooster Cogburn*, Wayne plays a character who was on a raft with a load of nitroglycerin. While he was facing perilous rapids, he shouted to his co-star, Katherine Hepburn (who portrayed a devoutly religious lady), "Sister, if He (God) owes you any favors, now is the time to ask!" Well, God owes no favors to anyone.

Still, it is hardly the point that God merely has the sovereign right to set the terms of salvation. The *real* answer is that the need to come to Christ is a simple matter of logic. Because, once one understands the divine nature of Jesus Christ and how He came to dismantle the sin barrier between God and man, it should be obvious to all but the blind that salvation can be through Him alone.

Now let's first discuss the dual nature of Jesus Christ, since the actual answer is found in the magnitude of His being. The Scriptures teach that Jesus Christ was not just a mere man, as the Jews thought. For in Him, undiminished Deity merged with uncorrupted humanity. This mystery is called the hypostatic union. Like the Trinity itself (God in three Persons yet one being), it is a mystery greater than the human mind can fathom. Jesus Christ, who is the second Person of the Trinity, took upon Himself a full complex of human nature, yet somehow without division or confusion of the two. At times, Scripture emphasizes Christ's humanity, and at others, it highlights His transcendent Deity. For example, passages such as Philippians 2:5-8 and Hebrews 2:5-18 underscore Christ's humanity. Others, such as Hebrews 1:3, underline the fact that Jesus Christ is the exact representation of the Father's divine Nature. So, despite Jesus' full humanity, nothing belonging to Deity is lacking in Him:

> For it was the Father's good pleasure for all the fullness
> [of Deity] to dwell in Him. (Col.1:19) [brackets mine]

Thus, the bottom line is this: When you receive Jesus Christ, the God-man, you embrace His Father; when you reject Christ, you reject the Father Himself. That is why the Lord Jesus claimed:

> He who sees Me sees the One who sent Me. (John 12:45)

Hence, Jesus Christ represents a spiritual litmus test ... a touchstone of one's disposition toward God. The Son, one might well say, is the very clone of God the Father. When we come to terms with that reality, it will no longer baffle us why Jesus alone is the way, the truth and the life.

How could it be any other way? For since the Son is the mirror image of His Father, it is a logical impossibility to simultaneously turn to the Father and yet turn one's back on His Son. As we stated earlier, in the mystery of the Trinity, the Father, Son and Holy Spirit are three Persons yet one essence. Nobody can fully explain that; no analogy can "get its arms" completely around it. Yet it should be clear that one cannot take one member of the Trinity and reject another, any more than one can usually separate Siamese twins.

Next, let's discuss the other reason Christ is so essential in the redemptive equation.

Consider the fundamental barrier between God and man.

People overlook what the Bible teaches about the sinfulness of human nature and the unapproachable holiness of God. We must understand that God is not like some majestic mountain that can be approached at will. There is an impassable gulf separating a holy God and sin-corrupted men.

It is not His incomprehensible transcendence that forbids intimacy with polluted men; rather it is His all-consumptive purity, "for our God is a consuming fire" (Hebrews 12:29). His holiness would devour defiled sinners, just as the wild, raging gases of the sun combust and dissolve all that comes near. A holy God will no more tolerate pollution in His presence than we would accept a plate of food scrambled with manure. Thus, for those who want to approach God, sin has to be atoned for; the sinner has to be purified.

Oh, yes, our flippant modern culture has trivialized "sin." You know that for sure when sin becomes comedic ... when a city such as Las Vegas is proudly touted as "Sin City." Not something to lament, but to laugh at.

Nevertheless, sin lies at the bottom of every evil and torture that afflicts this suffering world. Every horror and sadness that you've ever seen or heard about traces its roots back to this dark reality. No question, sin is the lethal phenomenon that ultimately accounts for the presence and intractability of death and disease on this writhing planet. In addition, sin (that prideful, self-serving rebellion against God and His laws so endemic to human nature) is the spiritual pathology that estranges men from God, drives all those hideous wedges between neighbors and nations, and even alienates persons from themselves.

But before man can be reconciled to his Creator, the impassable barrier—man's estrangement from God due to sin—must be removed. Jesus Christ came to break down that barrier for all who receive Him by faith. The Father sent Him and Him alone as the Mediator between God and man. He is the one "bridge over troubled waters," an otherwise insurmountable gulf.

So then, people who think that any way to God ought to be good enough fail to grasp that God has declared all men, without exception, to be sinners (or transgressors). Lest there is any doubt about that verdict, read Romans 3:9-18, which informs us that, in the eyes of God, "… There is *none* righteous, not even one" [italics mine] (3:10). Thus, before God, man is nothing less than a cosmic outlaw. By nature, we are moral runaways and spiritual renegades.

Men may mock as they please, but ridicule is no escape from accountability. Sin is a big deal. The price will be paid. "For the wages of sin [or transgression of the Law of God] is death [that is, everlasting death] …" (Romans 6:23a) [brackets mine]. Because of the penalty of sin, all people everywhere stand condemned before God.

We can, if we like, smirk skeptically and say, "Hogwash!" to all that. But that dismissive sentiment is born of wishful thinking, not biblical inquiry. Just jumping on the bandwagon with a loud mob of other wishful-thinking unbelievers, hoping it's not so, does not make it not so. The Bible says *it is so*.

Now then, what other aspect of God's holiness demands that, before one can approach God, the penalty for sin must be satisfied and the sinner must be purified? It is His unwavering justice and moral perfection. That is why He will never grade this fallen race on a curve. As the saying goes, if we do the crime, we must do the time. The sinner must die—or someone must die in his or her place as a substitute.

However, this substitute cannot be just anyone. It takes someone totally unique and not of this world. It takes someone perfectly righteous to stand in for a guilty person. And it takes someone of *infinite* worth to stand in for *all* the guilty from the beginning of time.

And that, again, is where Christ's true humanity and perfect Deity comes in. For He is the only Being in the cosmos who satisfies those two requirements. Because in Him alone, we find an inscrutable union of a divine Being of infinite worth and a human being of absolute moral perfection. He alone is the answer to the penalty of sin.

For those who receive Christ, His self-sacrifice on the Cross cancels the penalty of sin forever. The sprinkling of His precious blood, so to speak, applied to those who trust in Him, cleanses them forever. Once the "house" has been purified, then the Spirit of God can enter our space and take up abode in the believer. Through His indwelling Spirit, we then become sacred (organic) temples of the living God (Ez. 36:25-27, 1 Pe. 2:4-5).

But none of this can happen without Christ and the application of the benefits of His atonement.

At the risk of seeming to trivialize (by our language) an encounter with the living God, can anyone imagine that, when men give account, God will simply throw up His hands and say, "Ah, let's not slice it so thin! It really doesn't matter now. Honest mistake. We'll dance with who brung ya." That is a pipe dream. Don't fall for it.

Again, can anyone imagine the Father, who sent His beloved Son and exposed Him to so much humiliation and suffering for our redemption, declaring in the end to those who spurned Him and followed other paths, "Hey, it's OK. At least you were religious." That just won't happen.

Religion is like paper currency. Whether or not it has any value depends on what's behind it. As we know, currency not backed by gold is worthless. So religion without Christ is worthless.

If having "religion" was good enough, why would Jesus command His disciples to go into the entire pagan world and make disciples of all nations if, in the end, it would all come out in the wash anyway?

So then, we see that if we start with the Scriptures, OT or NT, one has to acknowledge the finality of Jesus Christ.

How Did God Accept People Before Christ Came?

Now we will address my friend Mary's next question. To begin, we must explain *how* God accepted people before the advent of Christ.

It is apparent that OT believers could *not* have placed their personal faith in Christ, who had not yet appeared. Yet, it is also clear that many men and women in the OT period trusted in God and were accepted by Him as His own.

This fact is illustrated by multiple examples in Hebrews 11. There, the author scrolls through a veritable spiritual "Hall of Fame," cataloguing a long list of spiritually heroic OT personalities who, as exemplars of faith in God, were accepted and rewarded by Him.

Even so, let me demonstrate that these OT believers' acceptance by God depended on Christ as much as ours.

How is that?

Remember, as we discussed earlier, how the Apostle Paul declared his countrymen's pursuit of a works-based righteousness futile? Well, that principle is a *constant* in God's acceptance of those who approach Him in *any* era.

You see, in any age, men who approach God are accepted on the basis of His "grace … through faith … not as a result of works, so that no one may boast [in one's own goodness and self-righteousness]" (Eph. 2:8-9) [brackets mine]. That principle has remained unchanged ever since the fall of Adam. Never has anyone been accepted on any other basis.

> And without faith it is impossible to please Him, for he who comes to God must believe that He is and that He is a rewarder of those who seek Him. (Hebrews 11:6)

> But the righteous will live by his faith. (Habakkuk 2:4b)

But what *has been* the variable in the redemptive equation is *how* God tested and proved one's faith in different eras. Yahweh, the God of Abraham, Isaac and Jacob, and the Father of our Lord Jesus Christ, challenged OT believers in various times to demonstrate their confidence in Him in different ways, as we see in Hebrews 11.

But Where is Christ in the Old Testament Scheme of Salvation?

Since faith, without the atoning provision of Jesus Christ, is null and void, how did God accept OT believers?

Here's the key: In OT times, the faith of men *looked forward* to God's pardoning provision in Christ; in the NT era, however, our faith *looks back* to God's redemptive provision in Christ for our pardon.

How then did God teach men and women of old to look forward to the advent of Christ? It was through the ritual animal sacrifices that the Lord prescribed for OT believers, foreshadowing the ultimate sacrifice of Christ's shed blood on the Cross.

Even still, these sacrifices themselves could not pay the penalty for sin. For, as Hebrews 10:4 states, "… it [was] impossible for the blood of [mere] bulls and goats to take away sins" [brackets mine]. So, OT believers trusted in a gracious, merciful God by faith just as we do, as we saw in Habakkuk. (See also Gen. 15:6, Ro. 4:3, Ja. 2:23.) In their case, then, the only way He could legitimately pardon their sins was that, in time, He would make a truly just provision for passing over their guilt. That provision turned out to be the atoning death of their promised Messiah, as we referred to in Isaiah 53.

Therefore, their acceptance by God is also *through Christ* and depends every bit as much as ours on the benefits of His sacrifice.

Remember, God cannot and will not wink at human guilt. He will not wave off the capital penalty of sin, as we saw in Romans 6:23. Again, this God of love is also a holy God. And perfection in justice is one aspect of His holiness. That is why the just penalty for sin must be satisfied. Otherwise, one of

God's moral perfections would be compromised. *That* will never happen.

Thus, to demonstrate His love on the one hand and His justice on the other, Jesus Christ resolved the tension. Stepping into history as our voluntary substitute, the Son of God became also a son of man and, at the appointed time, paid the penalty for our sin to the last drop of His precious blood.

What is Another Analogy for the Plan?

One might say, in a manner of speaking, that God accepted OT believers *on credit* in divine anticipation of Christ's coming. Whenever OT people evinced faith in Him *on His terms*, God extended to them, if we might put it so, a legal line of credit in covering the price of their sins. This upfront guarantee allowed God in all justice to receive them while temporarily overlooking or passing over their guilt. The full payment was on the way, so to speak.

Thus, "… when the fullness of time came, God sent forth His Son …" (Gal. 4:4a), and "… by the predetermined plan and foreknowledge of God …" (Acts 2:23a), Jesus came into the world as "… the one mediator between God and men …" (1 Tim. 2:5b). He sacrificed His life on a Roman cross as "… the propitiation [i.e., legal satisfaction] for our sins; and not for ours only, but also for those [sins] of the whole world" (1 John 2:2) [brackets mine].

Therefore, the atoning efficacy of Christ's death *looks back* as well as *looks forward*. This is a major emphasis in the Apostle Paul's thought in Romans 3:24-26. There, he explains how people, both past and present, gain acceptance with God. Paul stresses the fact that we are all:

… justified [accepted as righteous] as a gift by His grace through the redemption which is in Christ Jesus; whom God displayed publicly [on a Roman cross] as a propitiation [i.e., legal satisfaction] in His blood through faith. **This [propitiation] was to demonstrate His righteousness [or perfect justice], because in the forbearance of God [in the times prior to Christ's advent] He passed over the sins previously committed;** for the [public and legal] demonstration, I say, of His righteousness [or perfect justice] at the present time [in seeing that the penalty for sin was duly exacted], so that He would be [at the same time seen as] just and the justifier of the one who has faith in Jesus [here and now]. [bolding and brackets mine]

Note carefully the bolded text above. When Christ died on the Cross, Heaven made a statement for all time. Lest anyone should imagine that God is forgetful or just shrugs off human guilt over time, God demonstrated that His justice is always sure, even if it should appear slow. In sending His Son to the Cross as our Substitute, He satisfied at last the requirements of justice. By this act, God served notice that when He accepted OT believers, before legal settlement for their transgressions had been made, that justice was not cheated. For Christ covered the gracious "credit line" extended to believing sinners in the OT period.

So, I say again, their entrance to God was through the same door as ours—Christ.

I will go even further. Not only was their acceptance by faith dependent on the same saving provision as ours (that is, Christ), but also for all practical purposes, their faith was focused on the same object (Christ) as ours.

How could that be, since OT believers never had the option either to receive or to reject Christ? Because they did what amounted to the same thing. As we saw earlier in the discussion about the Trinity, when they trusted in the invisible Yahweh, they trusted in the One whom the Son of God (Jesus Christ) came in the flesh to reveal to the world. Jesus put it this way:

> He who has seen Me has seen the Father. (John 14:9b)

And as the Apostle John summarized it in his prologue:

> No man has seen God at any time; the only begotten God who is in the bosom of the Father, He has explained [*exegesato*: to explain, interpret, describe, make known] Him. (John 1:18) [brackets mine]

An encounter with Jesus, I reiterate, is an encounter with God. To believe in God the Father is no different than believing in His Son; to reject His Son is to reject His Father. Jesus made no bones about the fact that the two are inseparable where faith is concerned:

> He who does not honor the Son does not honor the Father who sent Him. (John 5:23b)

Jesus also made it abundantly clear that "… he who rejects Me rejects the One who sent Me" (Luke 10:16c).

So, you see, when people in that era exhibited their faith in Yahweh, they, in effect, put their trust in the Son of God, the preincarnate Christ.

We come back then to the same conclusion: there is no bypassing of Jesus Christ enroute to God. Not then, not now. It is a logical impossibility. The *one God who is there* is the God and Father of Jesus Christ.

This brings us to the next topic.

What is the Status of Adherents of Non-Christian Religions?

What about Mary's final group of questions? How do we address the fate of people, reared in non-Christian cultures, who are attached to their native religions? Are they lost simply because they had the misfortune to be born in a part of the world where they would never learn about Christ? "That doesn't seem fair," people say. To hear their apologists tell it, followers of non-Christian religions are people who, in their own sincere way, are reaching out to God the best way they know how, according to the light they have.

This take on the spiritual posture of adherents to non-Christian religions is, according to the Scriptures, wildly distorted. Such a spin miscasts the reality of the situation. It presumes a level of religious innocence that biblical theology refuses to grant. That supposition, according to the Apostle Paul, is simply not the case. *In reality, whatever the appearances, their religions are not an effort to ascend to God, but a defection from God.*

For *God's* take on their religions, let's take our cues from Paul's discourse in Romans 1:18-32. According to Paul, they all know better—or at least at some point in their lives they did. This is why God is indignant.

> For the wrath of God is revealed from heaven against all ungodliness and unrighteousness of men who [note this!] suppress the truth [about God, that is] in unrighteousness ... (Romans 1:18) [brackets mine]

What, then, are non-Christians guilty of suppressing? It is the truth of God's attributes and nature. For this reason, Paul continues in v.19a, "because that which is known [innately] about God is evident within them ..." [brackets mine]. And it is because of this suppression of truth that God's wrath abides on them.

Note the implication. Contrary to popular notions, non-Christians are *not* worshiping according to the light they have. The fact is, they are suppressing it *in unrighteousness.* They know better than they act, religiously speaking. The dim light they have is bright enough to hold them accountable before God.

How do we know that?

> … God made it evident to them. (Ro.1:19b)

How did they get it? Where did it come from?

> … **since the creation of the world His invisible attributes, His eternal power and divine nature, have been clearly seen, being understood through what has been made** [that is, the nature of God intuitively perceived from His creative works]. (Romans 1:20a) [bolding and brackets mine]

All over the world, from time immemorial, men have enjoyed the benefit of a certain amount of divine knowledge. We call it "natural" revelation. This real but primitive knowledge of God is imprinted on the human consciousness through God's handiwork in creation itself.

> The heavens are telling of the glory of God; And their expanse is declaring the work of His hands. (Ps.19:1)

However limited in scope, this light is sufficiently clear to test the attitude of men about their Creator. The net result of their rejection of the light they have is that, Paul emphasizes, "… they are without excuse" (Romans 1:20c).

So, that false face of religious innocence or sincerity won't play in Heaven. Those who gravitate to other religions don't have a leg to stand on. Instead, they failed to take advantage of the residual knowledge God provided as a basis for seeking Him and went another way. Their ignorance, then, is not a matter of innocence; it is really an indictment.

Here's the history of false religions over and over again:

> For even though they knew God [at some point], they did not honor Him as God [that is, seek and worship Him according to the light they had] or give thanks [to Him at least], but they became futile in their speculations [religious and otherwise], and [as always happens when people turn away from light] their foolish heart was darkened. Professing to be wise, they became fools [what an indictment of non-Christian religions!] and exchanged [in their dive into idolatry] the glory of an incorruptible God for an image in the form of corruptible man and of birds and four-footed animals and crawling creatures. (Romans 1:21-23) [brackets mine]

Let's understand this: Sincerity means nothing before God. For instance, we have all heard of mass murderers who sincerely believe that the voice of God commanded them to slaughter innocent people. In the same way, sincerity is no excuse for men to exchange the glory of God for idols of their own making.

Again, the Apostle proclaims that their attachment to off-brand religions is culpable because they trashed whatever natural light God had given them. The truth is, they simply had no appetite for the kind of God to which that light points. They wanted to reinvent God to suit their own fancies. So, turning their backs on the light they had, their minds were darkened. Off they went into Hell's follies. Now they are without excuse.

Of course, people may beg to differ. That is their right, even if they are wrong. Just as it is their right to believe that O.J. Simpson was innocent of two savage murders. But we take our stand on divine authority.

Still, someone (like Mary) might object that it doesn't seem fair for people to be condemned when they never had any opportunity to accept or reject Christ. It seems like they should at least be confronted with that choice, some might argue.

That objection misses the point above.

You see, non-Christians have, in effect, been tested about their attitude toward Christ, even if they have never heard of Him.

"How could that be?" someone will protest.

Take this illustration. Imagine that I am on a humanitarian mission to Ethiopia and I come across a starving person. At the moment, all I have with me is a bag of raw broccoli. Urgently I reach in, take out one little piece and place it in the outstretched hand of the desperate victim. Amazingly, the dying person spews the broccoli out of his mouth as if it were poison, even though he is at the point of starvation.

Now consider this: Even though I failed to hand him enough food to save his life, I did give him an adequate amount, in a manner of speaking, to "condemn" him, should he reject it. If he perishes, it will not happen because I refused him enough broccoli to save his life; rather, he will die because he hates it. He proved that.

So it is with the redeeming light of God. Even if one's exposure to spiritual light is minuscule, it is still of the same moral quality. In other words, broccoli is broccoli, no matter the amount. What that means is that *a little tad will test us.* Thus, even though creation itself sheds less light on the knowledge of

God than the Gospel itself, it is still of one cloth with the most perfect Light revealed in Jesus Christ (John 9:5).

I reiterate, if I don't like a little sprout of broccoli, there is no reason in the world to dump the whole bag on me. My taste for the little bit defines my taste for the whole. Likewise, God does not need to reveal the entire Gospel of Christ to unbelievers in order to assess their response. *For their response to the flicker of light they already possess exposes their aversion to more of the same.*

Also, factor in this biblical reality:

> … you will find [God] if you search for Him with all your heart and all your soul. (Deut. 4:29b) [brackets mine]

> You will seek Me and find Me when you search for Me with all your heart. (Jeremiah 29:13)

This truth pertains to God's dealings at all times with all people. God never turns His back on an honest seeker. Never. If anyone anywhere in the world truly seeks for Him … really wants to know Him on His own terms … God *guarantees* that person will find Him.

From this principle, we can deduce that if people fail to find God, their failure is proof positive that they did not really seek God with *all* their heart—no matter how much they protest otherwise. The problem is not a matter of cultural or generational ignorance; the fault lies in the disposition of one's heart toward God.

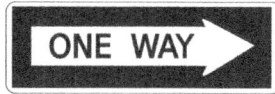

ONE WAY

Summary

Now let's pull the threads together.

1) Are there many roads to God?

No. There is one and only one. That road runs through and to Jesus Christ.

*2) Is our message **exclusive**?*

Not at all. In fact, our message exemplifies inclusion because, as we discussed, it offers salvation to all mankind, "for WHOEVER WILL CALL UPON THE NAME OF THE LORD WILL BE SAVED" (Romans 10:13).

3) Why must God be so rigid about receiving Christ?

It's not a matter of rigidity. It's a matter of logic. Since Christ is the only mediator between God and man, and is one with the Father, it is a logical impossibility to bypass Christ enroute to the Father.

4) What about the status of people born before the time of Christ?

OT believers were saved by grace through faith, just as we are. The difference is that their pardon was *in prospect* of Christ's atoning sacrifice; ours is *in retrospect.* In both cases, our salvation is founded squarely on the Son of God, who manifested the love of Yahweh through His redemptive sacrifice on the Cross.

5) What about the followers of non-Christian religions in our day who have never learned of Christ? Will God still condemn them?

Those who have never heard of Christ will not be condemned for rejecting Him directly; rather, they will be condemned for rejecting the light they already have.

The Bible teaches us that non-Christian religions suppress the light that God has imprinted on the human consciousness by means of natural revelation. Man's false religions betray 1) the need for man to fill a certain God-sized cavity and 2) his universal awareness of God. Nevertheless, his chronic and ubiquitous idolatry is a defection from the one true God. Like Cain, the first son of Adam and Eve (Gen. 4:1-26, Jude 1:11), they demonstrate a preference for demonically inspired gods or distortions of Yahweh.

6) Finally, are we Christians intolerant of other religions?

No. Biblically informed Christians excel in loving all people, even those who hate them.

Tolerance, however, does not mean accepting or condoning what other people believe. If that were true, *everyone* by that definition is intolerant and the word becomes meaningless.

Actually, *tolerance means putting up with views and actions we disagree with. Tolerance is conceding someone the right to be wrong.*

Nobody does that better than disciples of our Lord Jesus Christ. Even still, tolerance does not deprive us of the right or relieve us of the responsibility to persuade someone, if possible, that his or her views or actions are in error. Otherwise, we would have to lump every conscientious parent, teacher, coach and counselor in the category of the grossly intolerant. What thinking person would label the corrections of these pillars of society as narrow-minded or bigoted? And what about heroic firemen who selflessly warn others about their impending demise?

In the same way, we Christians try to persuade people in danger of losing their lives to wake up and get out of the burning building, so to speak, before it is too late. Sounds for the world like a benevolent project to me.

Curiously, critics are quick to tar Christians with the "intolerance" brush, yet they refuse to apply it to themselves when the tables are turned. They do not acknowledge *their own* intolerance when they show contempt for Christians and disparage our beliefs. Is there something wrong with this picture?

Christians are *not* crusaders against other religions, though we do see their demonic origin. What we champion is Christ. "Therefore, we are ambassadors of Christ, as though God were making an appeal through us; we beg [the world] on behalf of Christ, be reconciled to God" (2 Cor. 5:20) [brackets mine].

Again, our mission is not to revile others, but to rescue them. We are not here to put people down, but to lift them to Heaven. Our duty as Christians is to awaken them and tell them to vacate the burning building, and if that loving alarm insults them, that is their problem. As ambassadors, our message to the world is not a matter of our personal choice. It is our Lord Jesus Christ's command (Mat. 28:19-20).

THE WAY

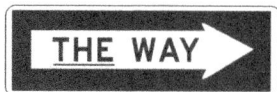

Appendix: How Do I Become a Christian?

The first step in becoming reconciled to God is repentance. When the Apostle Peter's Jewish countrymen asked him, "… what shall we do [to be saved]?" he answered, "… Repent, and each of you be baptized in the name of Jesus Christ for the forgiveness of your sins; and you will receive the gift of the Holy Spirit" (Acts 2:37c-38) [brackets mine]. As we noted earlier, to repent means to change one's mind and turn away from sin. Repentance is not separate from faith; it is the first act of faith.

Repentance

What specifically should we confess to God about our sinful mindset and actions?

1) We have suppressed the truth about God in unrighteousness (Ro. 1:18).
2) We have refused to believe in the One whom He has sent (John 3:18).
3) We have been sinners since birth (Ps. 51:5).
4) From God's perspective, there is no (moral) good in us whatsoever (Ro. 3:10). At every point of the Ten Commandments, we have transgressed His Law, either

in our inward motives or outward actions. We have selfishly pursued our own sinful ways rather than living for God's glory, for the Scriptures teach that we were created by Him and for Him (Col. 1:16).

5) Since there is no good in us, we are incapable of saving ourselves. As we noted in Ephesians 2:8-10, it is only by God's grace (His unmerited favor) through faith in Christ's atoning work alone that we are saved.

Baptism in the Name of Jesus for Forgiveness of Sins

What is Christian baptism? It is a ritual performed by immersing the new believer in water. It signifies one's repentance from the old way of life and commitment, by faith, to walk in Christ's new way. It stands for the entire response to God's call on our lives.

Does the ritual of baptism save us? No. The Apostle Peter relieves us of any such illusion when he clarifies this issue in 1 Pe. 3:21, "... baptism now saves you—*not the removal of dirt from the flesh but an appeal to God for a good conscience*—through the resurrection of Jesus Christ" [italics mine]. Thus, clearly he is talking about the crucial core of baptism—our faith, not the water. So then, baptism is a symbol of a Christian's faith and dedication, just as the physical altar where one takes the wedding vows becomes a symbol of marriage itself. For example, when we ask the question, "What year did you go to the altar?" we are not indicating that the act of standing at the altar makes one married. Rather, it is the heartfelt exchange of wedding vows that legally secures the marriage.

Again, it is only by faith in Christ's atoning sacrifice that we are saved. For the Apostle Paul makes it abundantly clear that "... by the works of the Law no flesh will be justified in

His sight" (Ro. 3:20a). By "the works of the Law," Paul means any human actions that are necessary for *or contribute to* our salvation. Of course, this would include baptism. In fact, Paul goes even further when he proclaims *twice* that anyone who teaches such a doctrine is eternally condemned (Gal. 1:8-9).

So then, to be baptized in the name of the Lord Jesus Christ is to confess from the heart that everything Jesus said about our need for salvation is true. It is also to confess *who* He is (God in the flesh) and *what* He has done for us (in becoming a man) in order to atone for and conquer our sins through His death on the Cross and resurrection from the dead. It is a pledge of faith, a submissive "Yes" to God's will for our lives. Therefore, our baptismal confession is far more than a mere intellectual assent to a set of propositional truths. For as James 2:19 reminds us, the demons also believe these truths and shudder.

The Scriptures teach that baptism also symbolizes our identification with Christ's substitutionary death on our behalf. But exactly what does that mean? The Apostle Paul explains in Romans 6:3 and 6, "Or do you not know that all of us who have been baptized into Christ Jesus have been baptized into His death? ... knowing this, that our **old self** [old sinful nature] was **crucified with Him**, in order that our body of sin might be done away with, so that we would no longer be slaves to sin [unable to please God and unable to live according to His prescribed will]" [bolding and brackets mine].

We need to further understand that when Christ died, His *legal* association with sin ended. In Romans 6:10, Paul says, "For the death that He died, He died to sin once for all; but the life that He lives, He lives to God." And why was Christ's death to sin necessary? Because "[God] made Him who knew no sin to be sin on our behalf, so that we might become the righteousness of God in Him" (2 Co. 5:21) [brackets mine].

What significance does this have for us? Since Christ's *substitutionary* relationship with sin is finished, so likewise, our connection with sin should be resolutely terminated. For Paul continues in the Romans passage, "Even so consider yourselves to be dead to sin, but alive to God in Christ Jesus" (Ro. 6:11).

Therefore, baptism symbolizes our identification with Christ's death to sin (that is, our dying to our own sinful desires) and our acknowledgement that, through His resurrection, we are now spiritually raised from the dead and empowered to live obedient lives dedicated to God. This is what Jesus meant by the phrase, "born again" (John 3:3). And this phrase leads us to the next subject, our participation in the very life of God.

Receiving the Gift of the Holy Spirit

When a person receives Christ as Lord and Savior, the Apostle Paul declares this: "... if anyone is in Christ, he is a *new creature*; the old things passed away; behold, new things have come" (2 Co. 5:17) [italics mine]. This truth answers the two most frequently asked questions when a person is on the cusp of receiving Christ. The first is the same as what the first-century Jews asked Jesus, "... What shall we *do*, so that we may work the *works* of God?" (John 6:28) [italics mine]. His answer was "... believe in Him whom [God] has sent" (John 6:29) [brackets mine].

The second question is "How will I be able to live a righteous life? I feel incapable of walking the straight and narrow path." So how does the Apostle Paul answer this question? First, he acknowledges that, before we come to Christ, "... the mind set on the flesh is hostile toward God; for it does not subject itself to the law of God, for it is *not even able to do so,* and those who are in the flesh cannot please God" (Romans 8:7-8) [italics mine]. But as we noted in 2 Corinthians 5:17, Paul explains that, when we come to Christ, it is by God's work of spiritual regeneration, through His Holy Spirit, that we become new creatures. Again, this is what Jesus meant when He said, "… unless one is born again he cannot see the kingdom of God" (John 3:3b).

In the OT, Ezekiel prophesied how God would accomplish this rebirth with the coming of the Spirit, transforming our hearts and enabling us, at last, to live a life pleasing to Him:

> Then I will sprinkle clean water on you, and you will be clean; I will cleanse you from all your filthiness and from all your idols. Moreover, I will give you a new heart and put a new spirit within you; and I will remove the heart of stone from your flesh and give you a heart of flesh. I will put My Spirit within you and cause you to walk in My statutes, and you will be careful to observe My ordinances. (Ez. 36:25-27)

First, we see in v. 25 that God cleanses us from all unrighteousness. (See also 1 John 1:9.) Next, we see that He transforms our hardened hearts into new hearts that are spiritually responsive when He implants His Spirit into our very beings (v. 26-27). It is this new heart, indwelt by the Holy Spirit, that enables us to walk according to His will, not in order to *earn* our salvation, but out of love and thanksgiving *for* our salvation.

For the first time, we not only *desire* to do God's will, but we have the power to pursue it. However, we need to recognize that when we come to Christ, we are, spiritually speaking, like newborn babies. Our spiritual growth is a process. We are not going to be able to hit the ground running and display instant maturity. But like a baby, all the potential for adult maturity is already present *and inevitable*. This growth occurs primarily through God's Spirit working through His Word. (See 1 Pe. 2:2.) The inevitability of our eventual maturity is why 2 Pe. 1:3-4 states:

> … His divine power has granted to us **everything** pertaining to life and godliness, through the true knowledge of Him who called us by His own glory and excellence. For by these He has granted to us His precious and magnificent promises, so that by them you may become partakers of the divine nature, having escaped the corruption that is in the world by lust. [bolding mine]

Thus, Peter promises that through God's divine power (His indwelling Spirit), we will participate in the very life of God. This does not mean that *we* will become gods, but that our lives will be permanently connected to God's eternal power. (See Eph. 1:18-21.) Because we will be *finally* fulfilling the purpose for which we were created, our core emptiness will be filled and the thirst of our lives quenched:

> … Jesus stood and cried out, saying, "If anyone is thirsty, let him come to Me and drink. He who believes in Me, as the Scripture said, 'From his innermost being will flow rivers of living water.'" But this He spoke of the Spirit, whom those who believed in Him were to receive … (John 7:37b-39a)

If you have decided to receive Christ, please contact us at Lake Bible Church — (503) 699-9840. For further help in growing in Christ, visit www.thefinalwordradio.com.

DOWNLOAD DAILY BIBLE TEACHING

TheFinalWordRadio.com

The Final Word is a daily Bible-teaching radio program from Pastor Jim Andrews of Lake Bible Church in Lake Oswego, Oregon. It currently airs in Portland, Oregon, and Pittsburgh, Pennsylvania. However, we hear from listeners all over the world who listen in via our web site.

Pastor Jim typically teaches through the books of the Bible in a verse-by-verse expositional style. Past messages are available in the podcast archive. We currently have available expositions of thirty books of the Bible, as well as six topical studies, with more studies added annually. We encourage you to take advantage of this extensive, free resource as you endeavor to understand and apply Scripture to your daily life.

Our contact information is:

The Final Word
4565 Carman Drive
Lake Oswego, Oregon 97035

(503) 699-9840
info@thefinalwordradio.com

ABOUT THE AUTHORS

Jim Andrews, senior pastor of Lake Bible Church in Lake Oswego, Oregon, is the author of *Polishing God's Monuments, A Life Worth Dying For, Marriage Without Remorse, and Dispatches from the Front Lines* (all available on www.jim-andrews.org). His degrees are in Journalism, New Testament Literature and Exegesis, and Classics. Prior to assuming his shepherding role at Lake, he taught for 21 years in Bible college and seminary. Pastor Andrews teaches a weekday Bible radio program, *The Final Word*, which he founded in 2002. Jim and his wife Olsie, have two married children, Kristi and Juli, and two married grandchildren, Alex and Ashley.

Juli Andrews Grose is the younger daughter of Jim and Olsie Andrews. She earned her undergraduate degree in Piano Performance from Wheaton Conservatory of Music, where she met her husband, Paul, who was also a Piano Performance Major. Paul also added a degree in Ethnomusicology in hopes that they could use their musical gifts for evangelistic purposes on the mission field. However, they were both struck with ME (myalgic encephalomyelitis, a.k.a. chronic fatigue syndrome) shortly thereafter, resulting in severe illness, pain and disability. Their story is recounted in Jim's first book, *Polishing God's Monuments: Pillars of Hope for Punishing Times*.

God has used her parents' influence, Jim's Bible teaching, and this devastating trial to instill a profound dependence upon and love for God's Word. Since Juli has been almost completely bedbound for most of her illness, she has been given the opportunity, within her limitations, to uniquely focus on listening to the expositional teaching of the Bible. She dictated her contributions and edits for *Finality* to Paul, who has been the editor for several of Jim's books.